D0582096

Purple Ronnie's

Little Thoughts about

MUMS

❁

by Purple Ronnie

First published 2003 by Boxtree
an imprint of Pan Macmillan Ltd
Pan Macmillan, 20 New Wharf Road, London N1 9RR
Basingstoke and Oxford
Associated companies throughout the World
www.panmacmillan.com

ISBN 0 7522 6485 0

A CIP catalogue record for this book is available from
the British Library.

Text by Giles Andreae
Illustrations by Janet Cronin
Printed and bound in Hong Kong

a poem for

My Mum

Being a mum is a difficult
job
That's not always easy
to do
But if I could choose the
best Mum in the world
I know I would go and
pick you

Warning:-

No-one can embarrass
you as brilliantly as
a Mum can

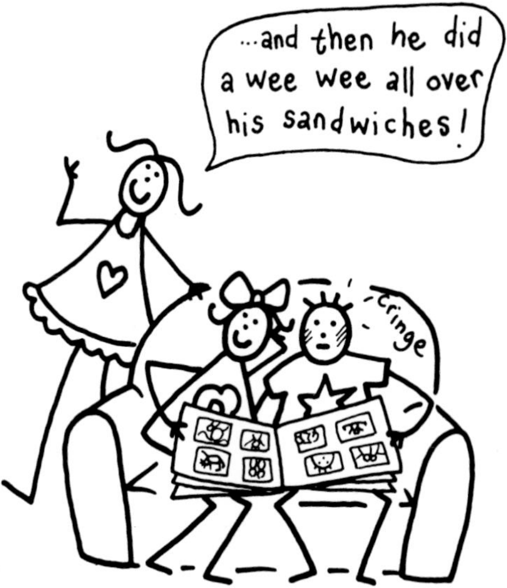
...and then he did a wee wee all over his sandwiches!
cringe

Remember :-

Sometimes even Mums need a little bit of spoiling

a poem for a
Lovely Mum

Mums can be embarrassing

And Mums can be a bore

But you're a really fab
one

And I couldn't love you
more

Mums and their Bodies

Some mums get completely obsessed by keeping fit. Others don't mind at all being a bit wobbly

Being Nice

It is always a good idea to be nice to your Mum. You never know when you might need her

a poem for a

Brilliant Mum

Some Mums can be batty

And can drive you round
the bend

But you're not just a
brilliant one

You're also a fab friend

Some Mums can't help
being critical when
they think they are
trying to help.

You must do your best
to ignore them

what do you think?
the carpet needs a hoover, your bed needs changing, and you ought to do the washing up
otherwise it's lovely!
in my new home

Remember :-

Being a Mum is one of the busiest jobs in the world. It is nice to give them a bit of help from time to time

brrrr

you →
chilling
out

a poem for

My Fab Mum

Why don't you put your
feet up
And take the day off too

Cos it must be very
hard to be

A Mum as fab as you

The biggest treat a
Mum can have is to
know that her little
darlings are happy

Mums and Driving

Even the most patient Mum can turn into a complete maniac when she gets behind a steering wheel

a poem for my
Groovy Mum

I wrote you this poem
to tell you

You're groovy, you're fab
and you're fun

And I really just wanted
to thank you

for being a wonderful mum

Beware

Mums are absolute experts at giving annoying advice

she's not really good enough for you darling
whisper
bye!
!
me fuming

Keeping in Touch

If you are miles away from home, even the shortest phone call can make your Mum unbelievably happy

shine

dazzle

a poem for a

Star Mum

Has anyone recently told
                    you

How totally smashing
                you are

If not here's a poem to
                tell you

That this person thinks
            you're a star

<u>Waking Up</u>

Who needs an alarm
clock when you've
got a Mum?

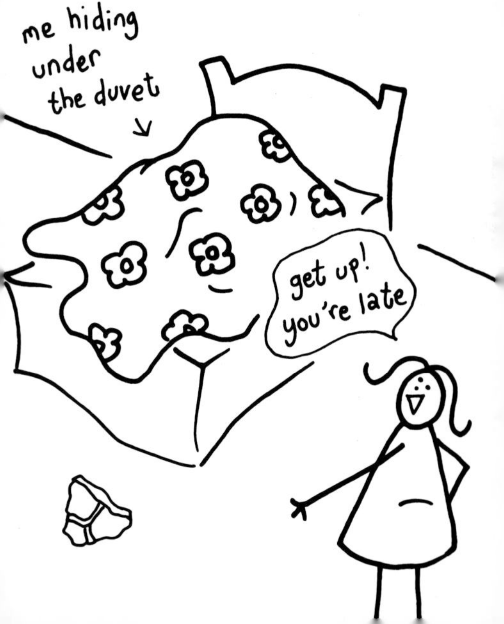
me hiding under the duvet
get up! you're late

Special Tip

Mums love nothing
more than a lovely
bunch of flowers

a poem for a

Magic Mum

Here's a little message

For a Mum who is the tops

It's to tell you that you're
magic

And to say I love you
lots

The great thing about Mums is that they're always there when you need them

I got chucked!
boo-hoo
sob
there there, never mind, plenty more fish in the sea etc. etc
YOU'RE CHUCKED

Some Mums never stop
thinking that you're
still their little baby

a poem for a
↓

Marvellous Mum

I know that it sounds
cheesy
But I'm telling you it's true
It's fab to have a Mum
Who is as marvellous
as you